J306.85

Please return/renew this item by the last date shown

worcestershire
countycouncil
Cultural Services

Our Global Community

Families

Lisa Easterling

Heinemann LIBRARY

www.heinemann.co.uk/library
Visit our website to find out more information about Heinemann Library books.

To order:
☎ Phone 44 (0) 1865 888066
   Send a fax to 44 (0) 1865 314091
   Visit the Heinemann Bookshop at www.heinemann.co.uk/library to browse our
   catalogue and order online.

First published in Great Britain by Heinemann Library,
Halley Court, Jordan Hill, Oxford OX2 8EJ, part of Harcourt
Education. Heinemann is a registered trademark of Harcourt
Education Ltd.

Editorial: Diyan Leake and Cassie Mayer
Design: Joanna Hinton-Malivoire
Picture research: Ruth Smith
Production: Duncan Gilbert

Origination: Chroma Graphics (Overseas) Pte Ltd
Printed and bound in China by South China
 Printing Company Ltd

ISBN 978 0 431 19105 8
11 10 09 08 07
10 9 8 7 6 5 4 3 2 1

British Library Cataloguing in Publication Data
Easterling, Lisa
   Families. - (Our global community)
   1. Family - Juvenile literature
   I. Title
   306.8'5

Acknowledgements
The publishers would like to thank the following for
permission to reproduce photographs: Alamy pp. **4** (Blend
Images), **8** (David Sanger Photography), **10** (Creatas), **12**
(David Noble Photography), **19**, **20** (Stefan Binkert), **23**
(Blend Images); Corbis pp. **5** (Karen Kasmauski), **6** (Ariel
Skelley), **7** (ROB & SAS), **9** (George Shelley), **11** (Nik
Wheeler), **13** (Dex Images, Inc.), **14** (Ariel Skelley), **15**, **16**
(Ariel Skelley), **18**; Getty Images p. **17** (Image Bank).

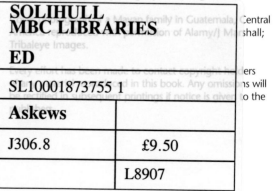

Contents

Families around the world

Families are people who are related.

People in families help each other.

Types of families

Some families are big.

Some families are small.

People in some families live together.

People in some families live apart.

Some families live in houses.

Some families move from place
to place.

What families do together

Some families work together.

Some families cook together.

Some families play music together.

Some families play games together.

Some families eat together.

Some families read together.

Some families walk together.

Some families ride bikes together.

Families have fun together.

What does your family like to do?

Family tree

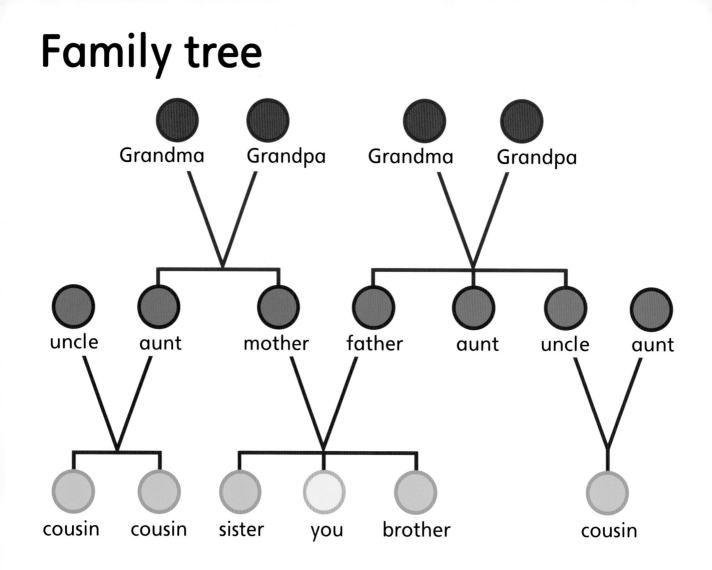

Picture glossary

related part of the same family

Index

Notes for parents and teachers

Before reading

Talk to the children about their families. Is their family big or small? Who has got the most brothers and sisters?

After reading

Family tree. Using the family tree on page 22 as a model, help each child to make their own family tree over three generations. Let the children take the tree home for adults to add information.

Family collage. Give children a selection of magazines and ask them to cut out pictures of families. Mount these on a wall display under the heading: "Families are different".

Family movement. In the hall ask children to stand in a circle. Tell them to first walk like great-grandfather with a walking stick. Beat a slow walking rhythm on a drum for the children to keep in time. Increase the beat and say they are to walk like a busy mum. Change the rhythm and style of walking for a crawling baby, an unsteady toddler, a sporty child, and so on.